I AM Confident

Name:

Copyright © 2021 Newbee Publication

ALL RIGHTS RESERVED

Thanks for Purchase
Scan QR code for more publications

This book may not be reproduced or transmitted in any form or by any means, electronic or mechanical, without written permission from the author.

I am a valuable human being.

I am a valuable human being.

I am a valuable human being.

I am a valuable human being.

I appreciate who I am.

I Appreciate who I am.

I Appreciate who I am.

I Appreciate who I am.

I Value myself as a person.

I Value myself as a person.

I Value myself as a person.

I Value myself as a person.

My future is bright.

My future is bright.

My future is bright.

My future is bright.

A little step every day.

A little step every day.

A little step every day.

A little step every day.

I enjoy little things in my life.

I enjoy little things in my life.

I enjoy little things in my life.

I enjoy little things in my life.

My future is positive.

My future is positive.

My future is positive.

My future is positive.

I am strong and can do hard things.

I am strong and can do hard things.

I am strong and can do hard things.

I am strong and can do hard things.

I am brave & have a positive mindset.

I am brave & have a positive mindset.

I am brave & have a positive mindset.

I am brave & have a positive mindset.

I am confident and beautiful.

I am confident and beautiful.

I am confident and beautiful.

I am confident and beautiful.

I am capable of facing my fears.

I am capable of facing my fears.

I am capable of facing my fears.

I am capable of facing my fears.

My friends and family love me.

My friends and family love me.

My friends and family love me.

My friends and family love me.

I am excited about today.

I am excited about today.

I am excited about today.

I am excited about today.

I am kind to others.

I am kind to others.

I am kind to others.

I am kind to others.

I have done my best today.

I have done my best today.

I have done my best today.

I have done my best today.

I will make good choices for myself.

I will make good choices for myself.

I will make good choices for myself.

I will make good choices for myself.

I am capable of anything.

I am capable of anything.

I am capable of anything.

I am capable of anything.

I am creative and intelligent.

I am creative and intelligent.

I am creative and intelligent.

I am creative and intelligent.

I can set goals and follow them through.

I can set goals and follow them through.

I can set goals and follow them through.

I am at peace with myself.
I am at peace with myself.
I am at peace with myself.
I am at peace with myself.
I am at peace with myself.

I embrace change and challenges.

I embrace change and challenges.

I embrace change and challenges.

I embrace change and challenges.

I embrace change and challenges.

I believe in my abilities.

I believe in my abilities.

I believe in my abilities.

I believe in my abilities.

I believe in my abilities.

I dare to be myself.

I dare to be myself.

I dare to be myself.

I dare to be myself.

I am accepting of others.

I am accepting of others.

I am accepting of others.

I am accepting of others.

I am worthy of love.

I am worthy of love.

I am worthy of love.

I am worthy of love.

I am unique and thoughtful.

I am unique and thoughtful.

I am unique and thoughtful.

I am unique and thoughtful.

I am optimistic and enjoy my life.

I am optimistic and enjoy my life.

I am optimistic and enjoy my life.

I am optimistic and enjoy my life.

I see the good in myself.

I see the good in myself.

I see the good in myself.

I see the good in myself.

I am going after my dreams.

I am going after my dreams.

I am going after my dreams.

I am going after my dreams.

I respect myself and others.

I respect myself and others.

I respect myself and others.

I respect myself and others.

I learn from my mistakes.

I learn from my mistakes.

I learn from my mistakes.

I learn from my mistakes.

I can overcome challenges.

I can overcome challenges.

I can overcome challenges.

I can overcome challenges.

I can overcome challenges.

I am resilient & can face adversity.

I am resilient & can face adversity.

I am resilient & can face adversity.

I am resilient & can face adversity.

I can seize life's opportunities.

I can seize life's opportunities.

I can seize life's opportunities.

I can seize life's opportunities.

I know my power.

I know my power.

I am deserving of my dreams.

I am deserving of my dreams.

I am deserving of my dreams.

I am deserving of my dreams.

I am keeping my body healthy.

I am keeping my body healthy.

I am keeping my body healthy.

I am keeping my body healthy.

I am keeping my body healthy.

I am keeping my body healthy.

I am inspiring others with my
unwavering confidence.

I am inspiring others with my
unwavering confidence.

I am inspiring others with my
unwavering confidence.

I am fearless.

I am fearless.

I am fearless.

I choose what I become.

I choose what I become.

I choose what I become.

I believe today will be a good day.

I believe today will be a good day.

I believe today will be a good day.

I believe today will be a good day.

I believe today will be a good day.

I believe today will be a good day.

I am surrounding myself with love.

I am surrounding myself with love.

I am surrounding myself with love.

I am surrounding myself with love.

I am surrounding myself with love.

I am surrounding myself with love.

I am grateful for life for all I need.

I am grateful for life for all I need.

I am grateful for life for all I need.

I am grateful for life for all I need.

I am grateful for life for all I need.

I am grateful for life for all I need.

I am focusing on my dreams.

I am focusing on my dreams.

I am focusing on my dreams.

I am focusing on my dreams.

I am focusing on my dreams.

I am focusing on my dreams.

I am a loveable honest person.

I am a loveable honest person.

I am a loveable honest person.

I am a loveable honest person.

I am a loveable honest person.

I am a loveable honest person.

I am a rainbow in someone's day.

I am a rainbow in someone's day.

I am a rainbow in someone's day.

I am a rainbow in someone's day.

I am a rainbow

I can make the world a better place.

I can make the world a better place.

I can make the world a better place.

I can make the

I can work through my struggles.

I can work through my struggles.

I can work through my struggles.

I can work through my struggles.

I am sincere & have good moral values.

I am sincere & have good moral values.

I am sincere & have good moral values.

I am sincere & have good moral values.

I control my own destiny.

I control my own destiny.

I control my own destiny.

I am a warrior.

I am a warrior.

I am a warrior.

I define my own success.

I define my own success.

I define my own success.

I define my own success.

I have a warm heart.

I have a warm heart.

I have a warm heart.

I deserve greatness.

I deserve greatness.

I deserve greatness.

I am fantastic & I am proud of myself.

I am fantastic & I am proud of myself.

I am fantastic & I am proud of myself.

I am fantastic & I am proud of myself.

I am motivated and focused.

I am motivated and focused.

I am motivated and focused.

I am motivated and focused.

I am wise and mindful of my actions.

I am wise and mindful of my actions.

I am wise and mindful of my actions.

I am wise and mindful of my actions.

I am tough enough to handle challenges.

I am tough enough to handle challenges.

I am tough enough to handle challenges.

I am tough enough to handle challenges.

My determination is excellent.

My determination is excellent.

My determination is excellent.

My determination

I make my own choices.

I make my own choices.

I make my own choices.

I make my own choices.

I bring my own sunshine.

I bring my own sunshine.

I bring my own sunshine.

I bring my own sunshine.

I am valuable to society.

I am valuable to society.

I am valuable to society.

I am valuable to society.

I can keep my chin up when
things are hard.

I can keep my chin up when
things are hard.

I can keep my chin up when
things are hard.

I forgive others for their mistakes.

I forgive others for their mistakes.

I forgive others for their mistakes.

I forgive others for their mistakes.

I look fondly upon memories of my past.

I look fondly upon memories of my past.

I look fondly upon memories of my past.

I look fondly upon memories of my past.

I am improving my confidence
every day in every way.
I am improving my confidence
every day in every way.
I am improving my confidence
every day in every way.

I have flaws, but I believe in myself.

I have flaws, but I believe in myself.

I have flaws, but I believe in myself.

I don't have complaints about my flaws.

I don't have complaints about my flaws.

I don't have complaints about my flaws.

I am happy to learn new skills.

I am happy to learn new skills.

I am happy to learn new skills.

I am happy to learn new skills.

I am happy and motivated.

I am happy and motivated.

I am happy and motivated.

I am in control of my mind and body.

I am in control of my mind and body.

I am in control of my mind and body.

I am in control of my

I am in

My thoughts remain positive.

My thoughts remain positive.

My thoughts

I am a wonderful person.

I am unique.

I am thankful.

I am a leader.

I love myself and others.

I am blessed.

I am courageous.

I am safe in my surroundings.

I am hopeful for tomorrow.

I am hopeful for tomorrow.

I am a great friend.

I am caring to others.

I am helpful and kind.

I accept myself for who I am.

I am able to learn from my mistakes.

I always keep my head up.

I feel good about myself.

I am strong and act confident.

I breathe in confidence and exhale fear.

I am confident in my abilities and skills.

My growth is a continuous process.

I am letting go of doubt and fear.

I am learning to trust myself.

I am working on my challenges.

I oversee my emotions.

I am proud of who I am.

I remember things in great detail.

It is easy for me to learn new things.

Every challenge brings me new opportunities.

I enjoy problem-solving & learning opportunities.

Mastering new knowledge makes me feel powerful.

There are no limits to what I can do.

I am not afraid of failing.

I am hardworking, and my efforts pay off.

I have a strong body and a strong mind.

My dreams are within my reach, and I will never give up.

We would appreciate it if you could give a review on google
For More Publication visit our website

www.newbeepublication.com

www.ingramcontent.com/pod-product-compliance
Lightning Source LLC
Chambersburg PA
CBHW081710100526
44590CB00022B/3723